COMPOSER SHOWCASE

HAL LEONARD
STUDENT PIANO LIBRARY

LATE ELEMENTARY PIANO DUETS

Tour for Two

SIX DUETS FOR ONE PIANO, FOUR HANDS

BY EUGÉNIE ROCHEROLLE

To Noah and Emma Rocherolle

ISBN 978-1-4234-9702-8

HAL•LEONARD®
CORPORATION

7777 W. BLUEMOUND RD. P.O. BOX 13819 MILWAUKEE, WI 53213

In Australia Contact:
Hal Leonard Australia Pty. Ltd.
4 Lentara Court
Cheltenham, Victoria, 3192 Australia
Email: ausadmin@halleonard.com.au

Visit Hal Leonard Online at
www.halleonard.com

CONTENTS

Desert Caravan

Secondo

By Eugénie Rocherolle

Moderato (♩ = 112)

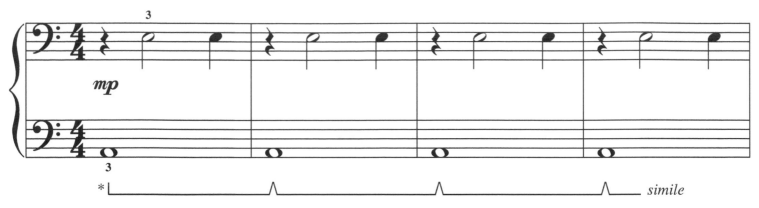

simile

pedal optional

Desert Caravan

Primo

By Eugénie Rocherolle

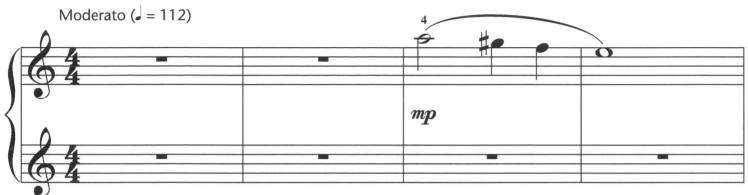

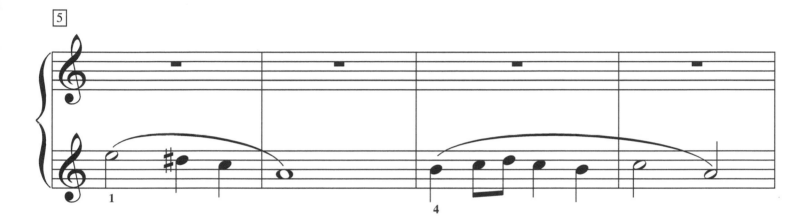

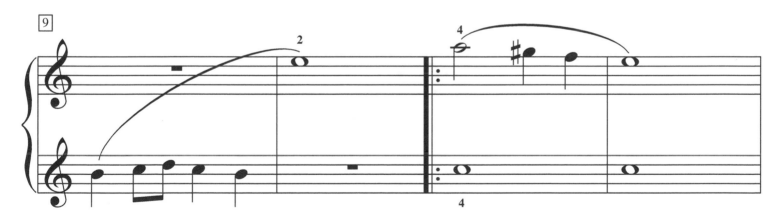

Secondo

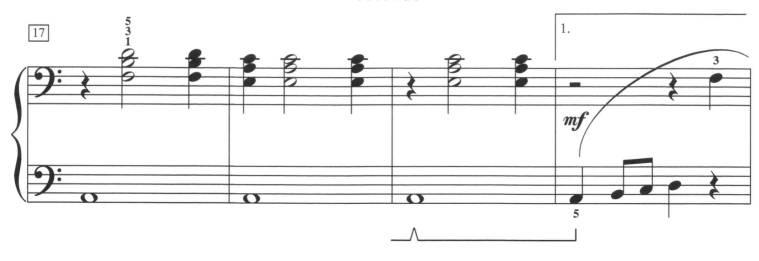

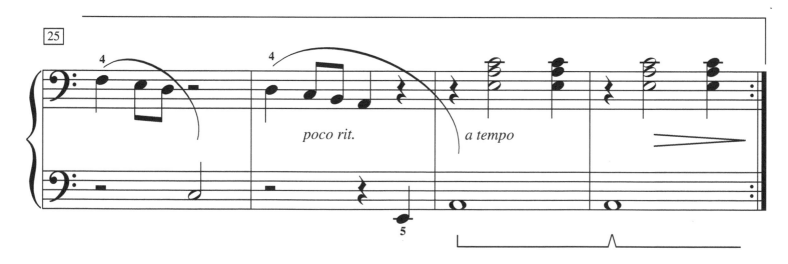

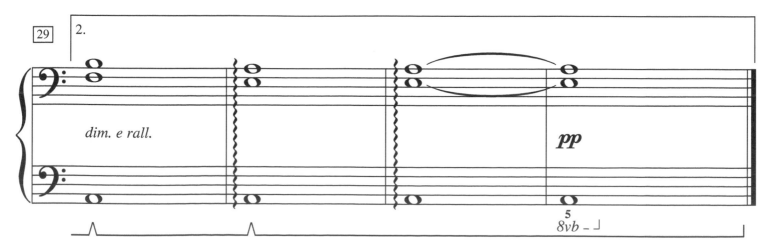

Primo

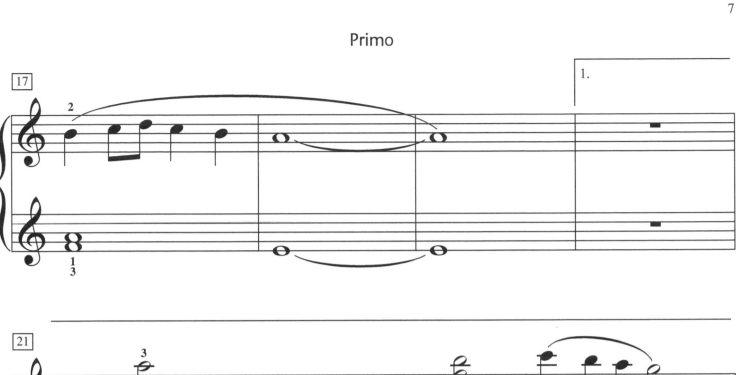

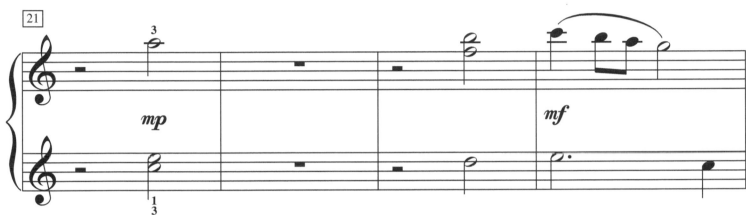

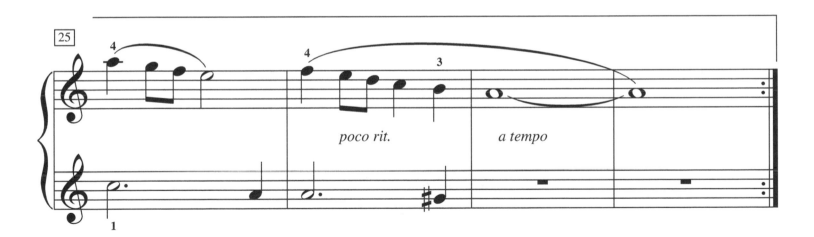

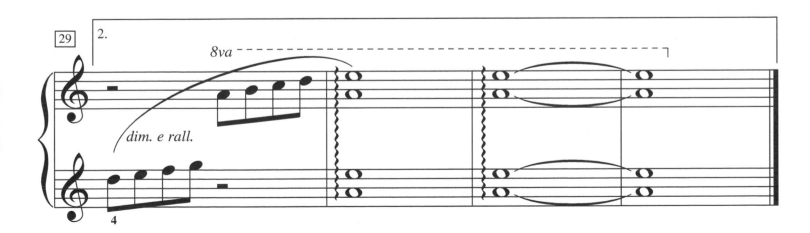

Highland Fling

Secondo

By Eugénie Rocherolle

Spirited, in 2 (♩. = 116)

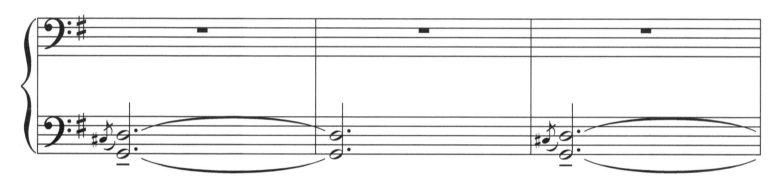

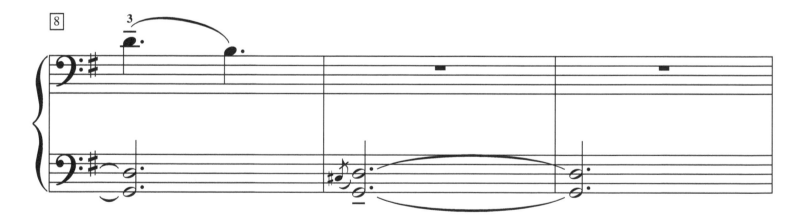

Highland Fling

Primo

By Eugénie Rocherolle

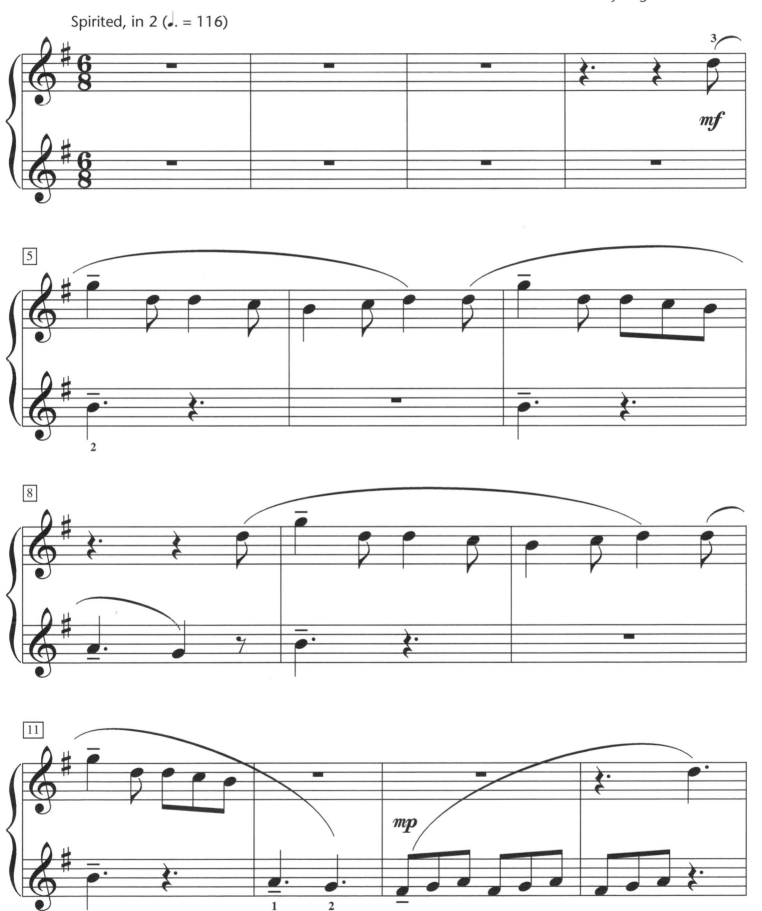

Secondo

Primo

12

Secondo

Primo

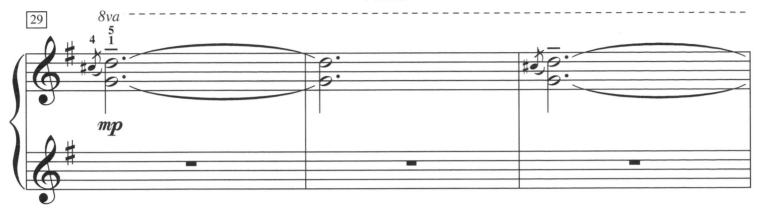

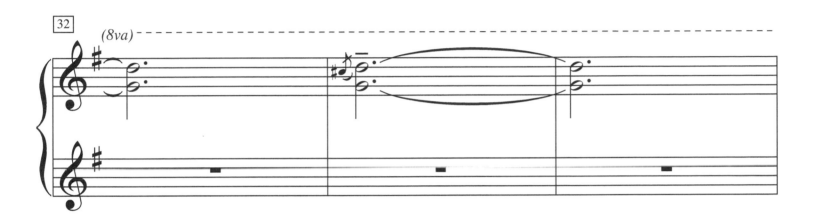

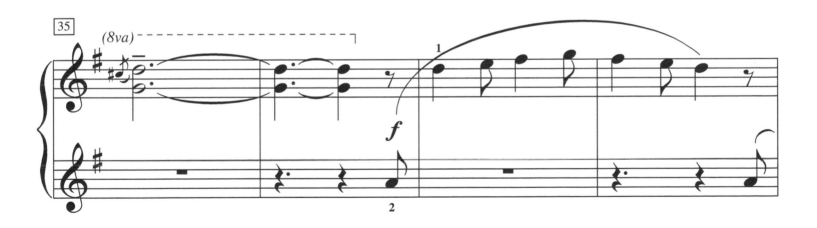

14

Secondo

Primo

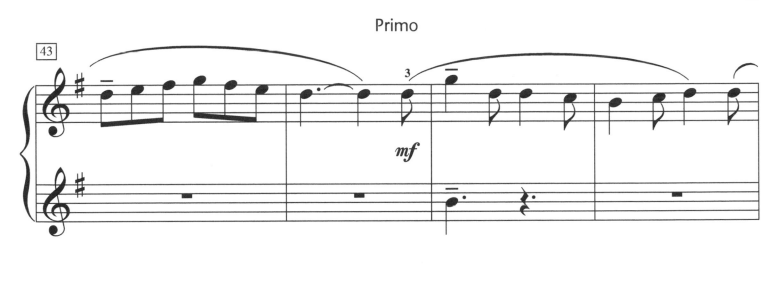

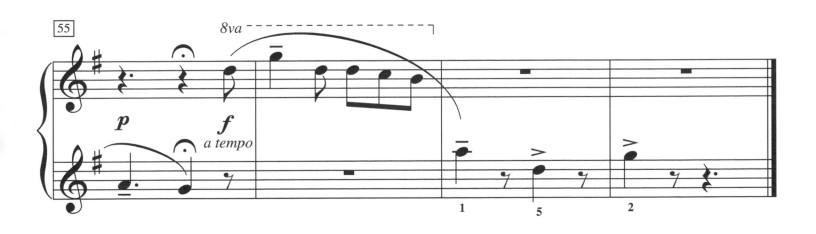

Latin Nights

Secondo

By Eugénie Rocherolle

Latin Nights

Primo

By Eugénie Rocherolle

Secondo

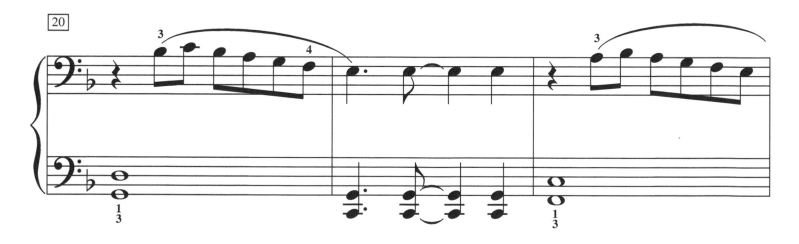

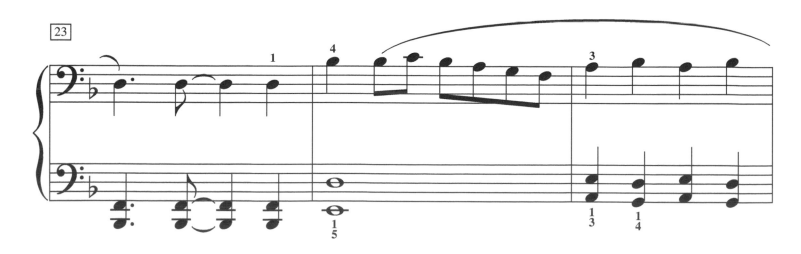

Primo

19

Secondo

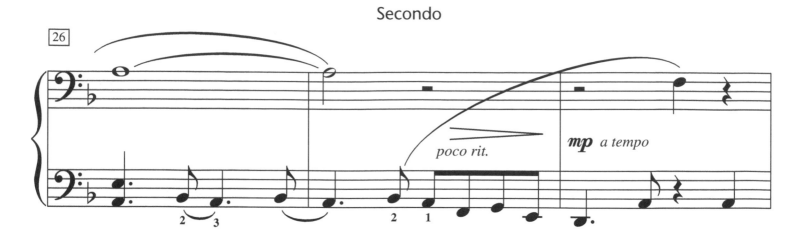

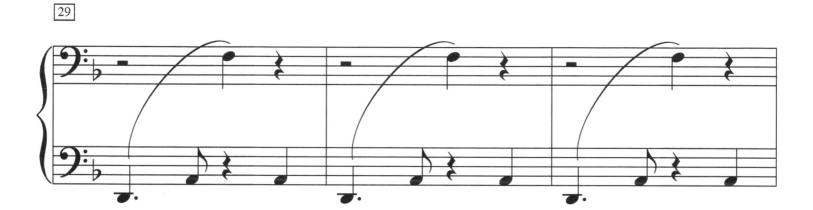

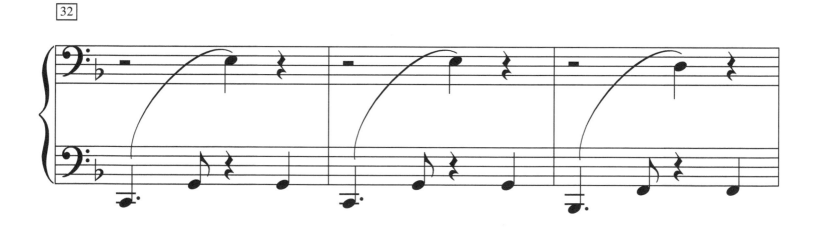

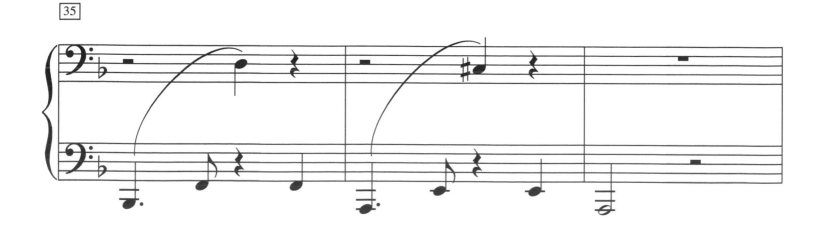

Primo

Secondo

Primo

Rickshaw Ride

Secondo

By Eugénie Rocherolle

Allegretto (♩ = 80)

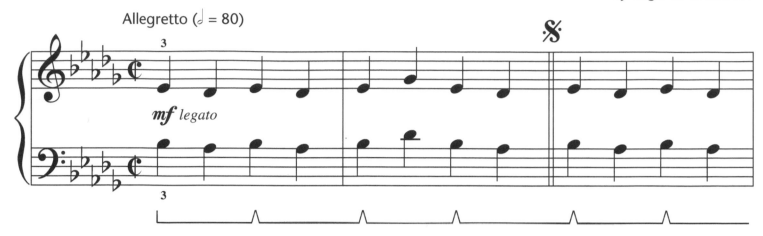

simile

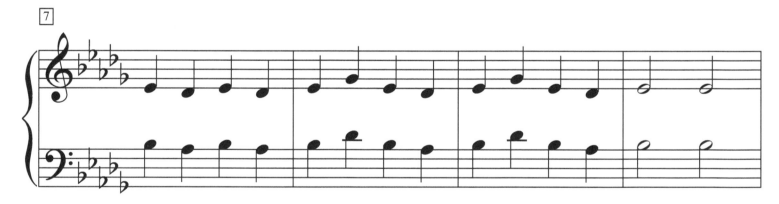

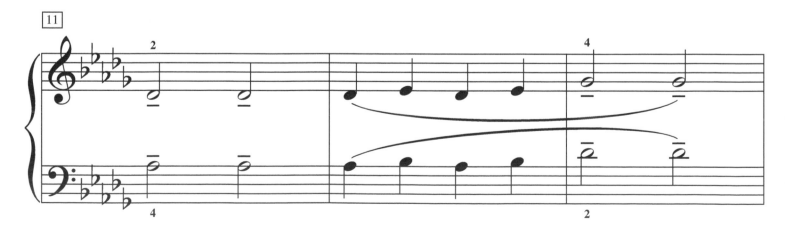

Rickshaw Ride

Primo

By Eugénie Rocherolle

Secondo

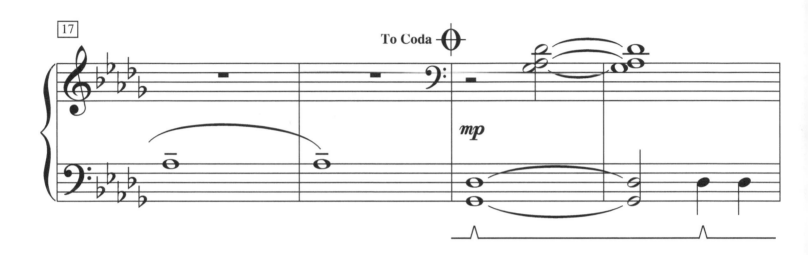

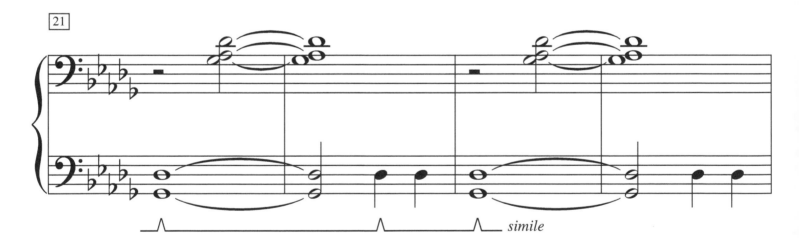

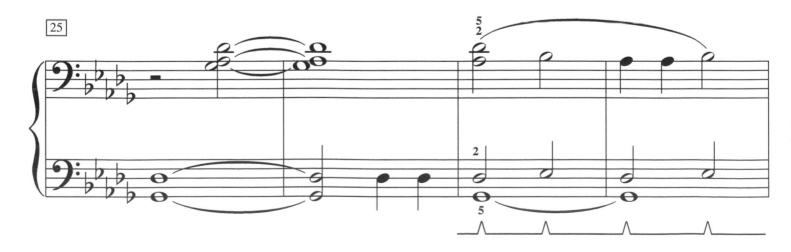

Primo

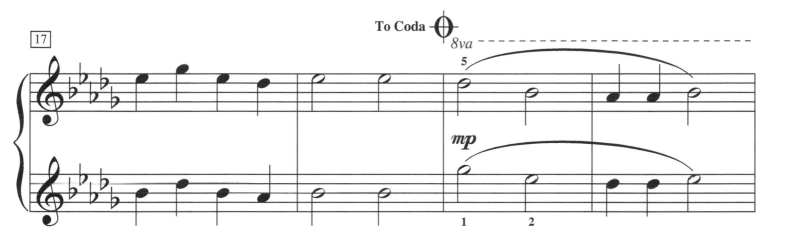

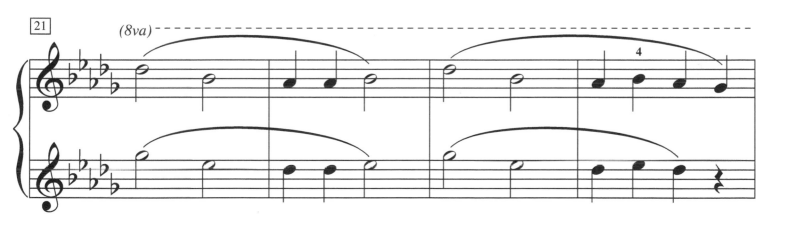

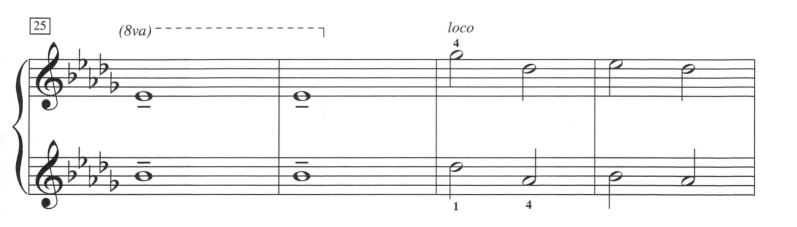

Secondo

Primo

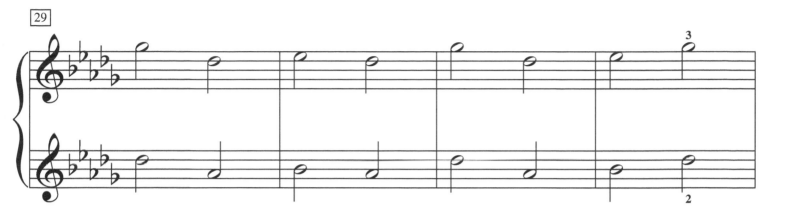

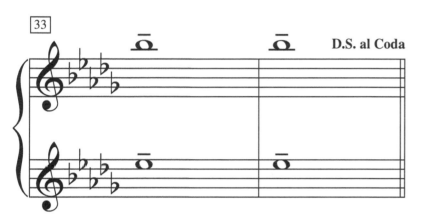

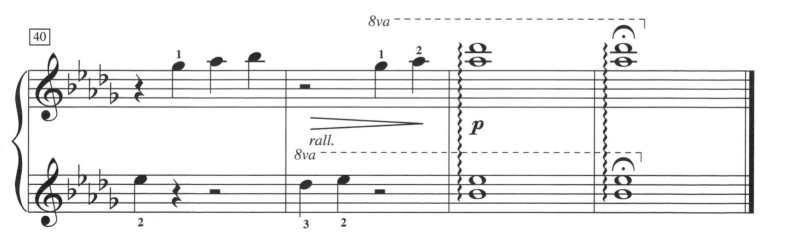

Russian Dance

Secondo

By Eugénie Rocherolle

Russian Dance

Primo

By Eugénie Rocherolle

Allegro, with gusto (♩ = 69)

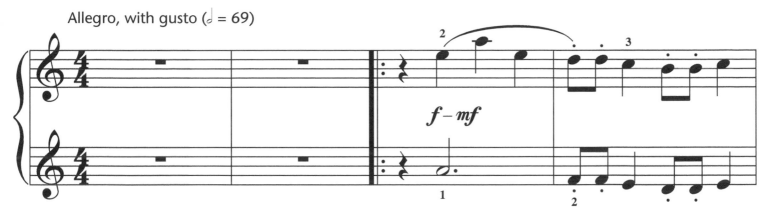

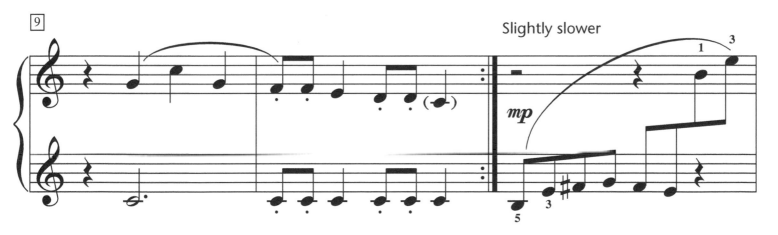

Secondo

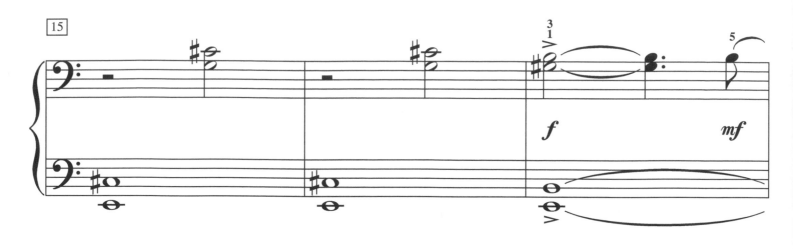

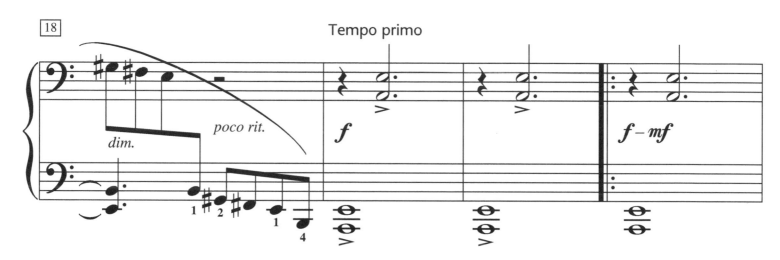

Tempo primo

Primo

Swingtime

Secondo

By Eugénie Rocherolle

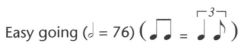

Swingtime

Primo

By Eugénie Rocherolle

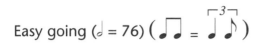

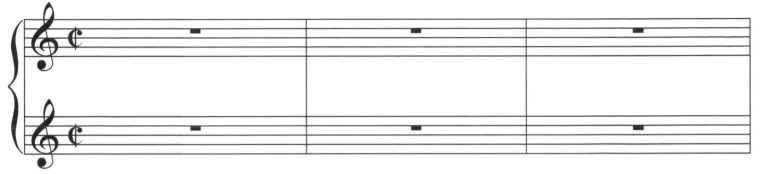

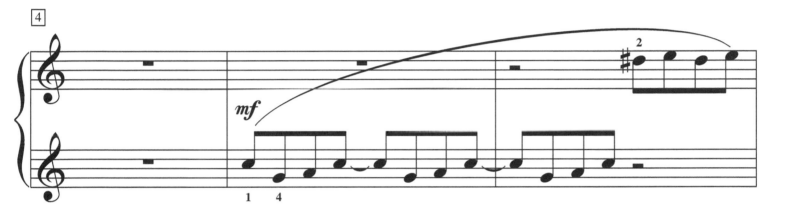

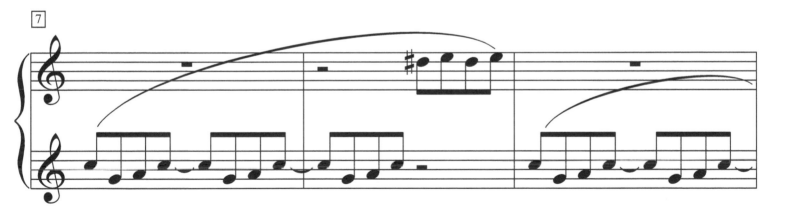

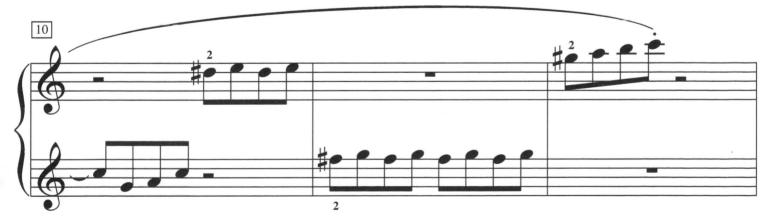

Secondo

Primo

Secondo

Primo

COMPOSER SHOWCASE
HAL·LEONARD STUDENT PIANO LIBRARY

This series showcases great original piano music from our **Hal Leonard Student Piano Library** family of composers. Carefully graded for easy selection.

BILL BOYD

JAZZ BITS (AND PIECES)
Early Intermediate Level
00290312 11 Solos......................$7.99

JAZZ DELIGHTS
Intermediate Level
00240435 11 Solos......................$8.99

JAZZ FEST
Intermediate Level
00240436 10 Solos......................$8.99

JAZZ PRELIMS
Early Elementary Level
00290032 12 Solos......................$7.99

JAZZ SKETCHES
Intermediate Level
00220001 8 Solos........................$8.99

JAZZ STARTERS
Elementary Level
00290425 10 Solos......................$7.99

JAZZ STARTERS II
Late Elementary Level
00290434 11 Solos......................$7.99

JAZZ STARTERS III
Late Elementary Level
00290465 12 Solos......................$8.99

THINK JAZZ!
Early Intermediate Level
00290417 Method Book................$12.99

TONY CARAMIA

JAZZ MOODS
Intermediate Level
00296728 8 Solos........................$6.95

SUITE DREAMS
Intermediate Level
00296775 4 Solos........................$6.99

SONDRA CLARK

THREE ODD METERS
Intermediate Level
00296472 3 Duets.......................$6.95

MATTHEW EDWARDS

CONCERTO FOR YOUNG PIANISTS
FOR 2 PIANOS, FOUR HANDS
Intermediate Level Book/CD
00296356 3 Movements $19.99

CONCERTO NO. 2 IN G MAJOR
FOR 2 PIANOS, 4 HANDS
Intermediate Level Book/CD
00296670 3 Movements................$17.99

PHILLIP KEVEREN

MOUSE ON A MIRROR
Late Elementary Level
00296361 5 Solos........................$8.99

MUSICAL MOODS
Elementary/Late Elementary Level
00296714 7 Solos........................$6.99

SHIFTY-EYED BLUES
Late Elementary Level
00296374 5 Solos........................$7.99

CAROL KLOSE

THE BEST OF CAROL KLOSE
Early Intermediate to Late Intermediate Level
00146151 15 Solos....................$12.99

CORAL REEF SUITE
Late Elementary Level
00296354 7 Solos........................$7.50

DESERT SUITE
Intermediate Level
00296667 6 Solos........................$7.99

FANCIFUL WALTZES
Early Intermediate Level
00296473 5 Solos........................$7.95

GARDEN TREASURES
Late Intermediate Level
00296787 5 Solos........................$8.50

ROMANTIC EXPRESSIONS
Intermediate/Late Intermediate Level
00296923 5 Solos........................$8.99

WATERCOLOR MINIATURES
Early Intermediate Level
00296848 7 Solos........................$7.99

JENNIFER LINN

AMERICAN IMPRESSIONS
Intermediate Level
00296471 6 Solos........................$8.99

ANIMALS HAVE FEELINGS TOO
Early Elementary/Elementary Level
00147789 8 Solos........................$8.99

CHRISTMAS IMPRESSIONS
Intermediate Level
00296706 8 Solos........................$8.99

JUST PINK
Elementary Level
00296722 9 Solos........................$8.99

LES PETITES IMAGES
Late Elementary Level
00296664 7 Solos........................$8.99

LES PETITES IMPRESSIONS
Intermediate Level
00296355 6 Solos........................$7.99

REFLECTIONS
Late Intermediate Level
00296843 5 Solos........................$8.99

TALES OF MYSTERY
Intermediate Level
00296769 6 Solos........................$8.99

LYNDA LYBECK-ROBINSON

ALASKA SKETCHES
Early Intermediate Level
00119637 8 Solos........................$7.99

AN AWESOME ADVENTURE
Late Elementary Level
00137563.................................$7.99

FOR THE BIRDS
Early Intermediate/Intermediate Level
00237078 ....$8.99

WHISPERING WOODS
Late Elementary Level
00275905 9 Solos........................$8.99

MONA REJINO

CIRCUS SUITE
Late Elementary Level
00296665 5 Solos........................$6.99

COLOR WHEEL
Early Intermediate Level
00201951 6 Solos........................$8.99

JUST FOR KIDS
Elementary Level
00296840 8 Solos........................$7.99

MERRY CHRISTMAS MEDLEYS
Intermediate Level
00296799 5 Solos........................$8.99

MINIATURES IN STYLE
Intermediate Level
00148088 6 Solos........................$8.99

PORTRAITS IN STYLE
Early Intermediate Level
00296507 6 Solos........................$8.99

EUGÉNIE ROCHEROLLE

CELEBRATION SUITE
Intermediate Level
00152724 3 Duets (1 Piano, 4 Hands)..............$8.99

**ENCANTOS ESPAÑOLES
(SPANISH DELIGHTS)**
Intermediate Level
00125451 6 Solos........................$8.99

JAMBALAYA
Intermediate Level
00296654 Ensemble (2 Pianos, 8 Hands)........$12.99

JAMBALAYA
Intermediate Level
00296725 Piano Duo (2 Pianos) $7.95

LITTLE BLUES CONCERTO
FOR 2 PIANOS, 4 HANDS
Early Intermediate Level
00142801 Piano Duo (2 Pianos, 4 Hands)........$12.99

TOUR FOR TWO
Late Elementary Level
00296832 6 Duets.......................$7.99

TREASURES
Late Elementary/Early Intermediate Level
00296924 7 Solos........................$8.99

JEREMY SISKIND

BIG APPLE JAZZ
Intermediate Level
00278209 8 Solos........................$8.99

MYTHS AND MONSTERS
Late Elementary/Early Intermediate Level
00148148 9 Solos........................$7.99

CHRISTOS TSITSAROS

DANCES FROM AROUND THE WORLD
Early Intermediate Level
00296688 7 Solos........................$8.99

LYRIC BALLADS
Intermediate/Late Intermediate Level
00102404 6 Solos........................$8.99

POETIC MOMENTS
Intermediate Level
00296403 8 Solos........................$8.99

SEA DIARY
Early Intermediate Level
00253486 9 Solos........................$8.99

SONATINA HUMORESQUE
Late Intermediate Level
00296772 3 Movements $6.99

SONGS WITHOUT WORDS
Intermediate Level
00296506 9 Solos........................$9.99

THREE PRELUDES
Early Advanced Level
00130747 ....$8.99

THROUGHOUT THE YEAR
Late Elementary Level
00296723 12 Duets......................$6.95

ADDITIONAL COLLECTIONS

AT THE LAKE
by Elvina Pearce
Elementary/Late Elementary Level
00131642 10 Solos and Duets..........................$7.99

COUNTY RAGTIME FESTIVAL
by Fred Kern
Intermediate Level
00296882 7 Rags.........................$7.99

LITTLE JAZZERS
by Jennifer Watts
Elementary/Late Elementary Level
00154573 Solos..........................8.99

PLAY THE BLUES!
by Luann Carman (Method Book)
Early Intermediate Level
00296357 10 Solos......................$9.99

Prices, contents, and availability subject
to change without notice.

HAL·LEONARD®
www.halleonard.com